I would like to dedicate this book to:

My Granddaughter Aubree D. Dockal

Crazy Paws Dog Rescue Group – Thank you for saving Pearl and other dogs through rescue, transport, and foster.

My beloved family members for all their love and support.

To all the heroes who can hear the cries of those who cannot speak: Thank you for all you do!

This story was inspired by my dog Pearl and her quirky antics of making her nightly pillow forts and her strange love of pickles.

"Laughter is timeless. Imagination has no age. And dreams are forever." -Walt Disney

Copyright © 2021 by Terry Bushey

Art director Bruce Giannini.

Hello! My name is Pearl.
I am a dog that was rescued by some kind people and adopted by my forever family.

Now that I am comfy and cozy in my new home, I found something I love to do!

I love making pillow forts and using my imagination to go on my very own adventures.

I use my nose to push the pillows, and my head to lift them up.

You know what I also love?

Pickles!

One day my mom gave me and my sister Sandy a pickle.

I loved it, but Sandy did not. She spit it out. Yuck! I would bring pickles into my pillow fort and munch on them.

Then, I would use my imagination and pretend my fort was a rocket ship that blasted off to the moon.

On the moon, there were trees that only grew pickles and dog bones with lots of squirrels that ran around for me to chase.

One day, I pretended my fort was a school bus for dogs. I would drive around and pick up my doggy friends.

Then we would go to a huge dog park with a pool.

There was sunshine, toys, bones, fresh green grass to roll in, tasty treats, and fire hydrants.

Sister Sandy came to keep an eye on us to make sure we stayed safe.

For my next adventure,
I pretended my fort was a
submarine and I was a scuba dog.

I swam with my new friends
a shark, dolphin, sea-horse
and some fish.

They showed me around their home
in the deep blue sea
and how wonderous it was.

I always wondered what it
would be like to fly an airplane.

With my imagination,
I was not only flying an airplane
but flying with a friendly dragon.

It was great looking down to see
the world from so high up.

People down below were
watching as we flew.

I loved the snow,
so I pretended my pillow fort
was a magical sled.

Sandy and I would
bundle up in our winter hats
and scarves and go sleigh riding
through the fluffy snow.

We saw many woodland animals.
A snowman came to life and waved
hi to us.

The trees were pretty covered in
snow. It was a winter wonderland.

I had so much fun using
my imagination.

I wondered if humans went on
adventures like me
and where would they go?

I felt adventorous,
happy, and safe in my fort.

At the end of the day,
my mom would call Sandy
and me to dinner.

Then, I would beg for more pickles
to bring to my fort.

Mom said:
"Do not eat too many pickles,
or you will get a bellyache."

I guess she was right.
My stomach felt funny,
and then I tooted and scared
poor Sandy.

As I lay in my comfy bed for
nighttime, I thought,
What a great life
eating pickles in my pillow fort,
as I fell asleep dreaming
of my next magical journey.

Author bio

Terry Bushey finds inspiration to write from her own sweet Pit Bull, Pearl, and has been involved in the betterment of dog and animal treatment for years through animal Law classes, Therapy dog training, reading and rescue dog groups. Fighting for the underdog. She is also the author "Pearl's Journey in Search of a Home."
Lives in Schenectady NY with her husband Mike Bushey and two dogs Pearl and Sandy.